Devils & Islands

Devils & Islands

poems

TURNER CASSITY

Swallow Press / Ohio University Press
Athens

Swallow Press / Ohio University Press, Athens, Ohio 45701
www.ohio.edu/oupress

© 2007 by Turner Cassity

Swallow Press / Ohio University Press books
are printed on acid-free paper ⊗ ™

15 14 13 12 11 10 09 08 07   5 4 3 2 1

The poems listed appeared first in the following periodicals:
"Before Clocks Were Digital": *Washington Square*
"Fashions of 1903": *Southwest Review*
"Crystal But Not Crystal Ball" and "Afterward": *The New Criterion*
"The Passion of 1934": *Atlanta Review*

I express my appreciation to Mike Haecker for trying to improve my
computer literacy in the preparation of this volume.

Library of Congress Cataloging-in-Publication Data
Cassity, Turner.
  Devils and islands : poems / Turner Cassity.
    p. cm.
  ISBN-13: 978-0-8040-1102-0 (acid-free paper)
  ISBN-10: 0-8040-1102-8 (acid-free paper)
  ISBN-13: 978-0-8040-1103-7 (pbk. : acid-free paper)
  ISBN-10: 0-8040-1103-6 (pbk. : acid-free paper)
  I. Title.

PS3553.A8D48 2007
811'.54—dc22

2007000333

"I wonder who began this treating of people as fellow creatures," said Charlotte. "It is never a success."

—I. Compton Burnett,
Manservant and Maidservant

Contents

Fantasia on Dummy Keys   1

Before Clocks Were Digital   2

After the Fall   3

Amazonas.com   5

Erich Wolfgang Korngold   6

The Last Newsboy   8

Hitting the Silk   9

Bargains Are by Definition Faustian   10

Opposing Colonizations   12

Robinson Crusoe to Capt. Dreyfus   13

Energy Crises   14

A Course in Sax Education   16

Production Values   17

Gowns by Adrian   19

The Garden of Yellow Jack   20

The Devil and Daedalus   21

Fashions of 1903   22

The Last Cigarette Girl   24

Dance   26

Free Trade in Mitteleuropa   27

Where Is Gutzon Borglum Now That We Need Him?   28

vii

Inventing the Subdivision   30

The Last Elevator Operator, or, Mr. Otis Regrets   31

Edith and Woody and Nancy and Ronnie   33

Fishers of Men   35

Unto Temptation   36

Guidelines for a Cover Illustration   38

Crystal But Not Crystal Ball   40

Models   41

The Last Chaperon   43

Update for Francis Joseph   44

The Passion of 1934   45

Administrating   47

One Third of a Triptych   48

Self-Guided Tour   49

Report of the Monuments Commission   51

Eclogue against Ecology   53

Soldiers Three in the Big Easy   54

Afterward   56

Devils & Islands

Fantasia on Dummy Keys

The harpsichord sounds like two skeletons copulating.

—Sir Thomas Beecham

The practice keyboard teaches only fingering.
Interpretation is beyond it. Lacking sound,
It will forgive wrong notes, not know an exercise
From Bach, if there indeed is some distinction. Mute,
It is the ideal medium for twelve-tone works,
If not the Chopin repertoire. Without response,
How judge of touch? Too firm? Too light? One must assume
Seducers learn and necrophiliacs do not,
Else why do spinet's key and quill go at it so?
Is Czerny a perversion? And if harpsichords
Seem musical cadavers, are the fringe who play
"Authentic instruments" grave robbers? They, in proof
Of scholarship as folly, preach that out-of-tune
Is what is called for. Vocal exercises—scales—
Employ an instrument whose authenticity
No one can doubt. A vocalise may have no words,
But is expression in a way dexterity,
Viewed, cannot ever be, although Franz Liszt might say
"*My* fingering could surely semaphore the deaf,
Who at recitals should be charged full ticket price."
To speak of heartstrings being plucked is retrograde,
As to both time and mechanism. Live hearts hammer.

Before Clocks Were Digital

Tonguing the brushes as they line a phosphorescent paint
Upon the dials that are piecework of their day,
The girls who presently will harbor cancer in the jaw
And die of it in more than one sense Time destroys.

In most of us a radium does not accumulate.
The numerals, however, do. They sum to what,
Subtracted by its twin the midnight hour, is nought indeed:
Zero of a departed beat, a darkened face.

As radium decays it goes to half-life, interim
Which we are not permitted. Half-life is for us
The half we call a coma. Greenish numerals that light
Insomnia, the hands that track it, are, dispersed

In time, the ghosts of those who painted them, or at the least
Their fit memorials—of application, tongue,
And talent, faint but glowing, form: the minute's trace prolonged
Beyond the minute, time-specific and yet more.

After the Fall

Created out of five-and-dimes,
The Woolworth sums up better times:

A Flemish Gothic 1910
Metropolis that might have been;

As, wholly 1932,
The Empire State, forever new,

Foretells a city so far seen
In drawings only, caught between

Prospectus and a backward glance
Toward Babylon. As we advance

The future takes on, more and more,
A look of follies gone before.

On every planner's mounting zeal
Hell's Kitchen comes to put its seal,

And where the streets of Haussmann go
Stood once the Walls of Jericho.

Above the airship mooring mast
The TV aerials broadcast,

Confirming that Count Zeppelin
Is where our Captain Kirks begin.

In fiction—pulp or subtler art—
In film, the silents at the start

And talkies after, Emerald
Or seven-gated, tightly walled

Yet welcoming, a citadel
No actuality can quell,

Our future is that city, myth
We are from childhood encumbered with.

Amazonas.com

Outside Manaus, not to disappoint the tours,
A number of the locals have obligingly
Gone native, hunter-gatherers in those locales
Not being numerous before the rubber boom
Annihilated all of them. The derelicts
In urban jungles stateside lack so safe a choice.
Feathers and piercings, body paint on them would seem
Survivals of the '60s, and increase dislike
That they incur, already great. Earrings are threats?
A naked savage is a homeless person, nude?
Curare is a savage's designer drug,
His head shop all too unequivocally that,
And any medicine of his, Alternative.
Headhunter, herbalist, ex-hippie growing old,
Have you as tourist trap, asylum, dead-end street
A jungle placable as this? All of your past
Tamed? Going native in its time was not PC.
It was admitting failure, just as, now, it's seen
As saving wildlife with a nose flute. Music puts
Also its spin on histories of peonage
In rubber gathering, an expiation based
On the offending firms' elitist theory
Goodyear will always be what makes the world go round,
And no town with an opera house can be all bad.

Erich Wolfgang Korngold

1897–1957

The perfect hero, perfect plot,
I did not live to score.
That would have meant, as like as not,
Techniques I used before,

But barer. Fewer upward sweeps
Among the strings; no harps;
Fanfares, but diatonic; leaps
Of key from flats to sharps

Avoided, save where, as with change
Of focus, they explain.
You cannot treat the Texas Range
And soundstage Spanish Main

In one tonality. But who
For hero, what the script?
A costumed Jüd in derring-do
Or Zarathustra stripped?

I am not Richard Strauss, alas,
Enjoying it both ways.
I am not sure it's greener grass
Or topiary maze

Or Herod's cistern I am in,
With Bette Davis soap.
And underscoring Errol Flynn
Needs certain skills to cope

Or one's own head is on the plate.
Not quite Jokanaan,
Contract renewed and up to date,
I notate on and on,

Who am an exile exiled thrice:
From city, era, tongue.
Of course, Vienna has its price.
I am no bard unsung.

Ex-prodigy I, you ex-star,
For our time left to be
We are in real life what we are.
The hero may be me.

The Last Newsboy

Not all of us grew up to be Irving Berlin.
There is not space to list the prisons we are in.

Pickpockets, hustlers, dealers, we became that news
We sold, if on the inside pages. Poor excuse

For urchin enterprise the vending that replaced.
A coin box is a generation gone to waste

And cannot give out change. Too often vandalized
To turn a profit, it becomes a recognized

Icon of inner city wreck, as in the past
We stood for rising expectations, if, at last

Our cry of "Extra!" covered the laments of lack.
The newsboy as the Chaplin Kid will not be back,

Having become decades ago the Dead End Kids
And then the Chaplin Tramp unfunny on the skids;

As now newspapers are. As AP, UP ebb,
Ex-buyer on my corner, see you on the Web.

Hitting the Silk

The golden parachute we really need
We need for the emotions. Severance
Can be, of course, itself a payoff. Bleed,
Heal, put behind . . . Still, falling from the chance

Of hurt through gentle letdown to a ground
On which to keep both feet has too a role.
Do not suppose, Fall Guy, there will be found
A second time such fancies of control

As once you had, or so bright element.
Long love, deep air, and if not silk and gold,
Haiku and kamikaze; loss, descent,
Downsizing. Wrap the final scarf, unfold

The chute, and skydive neat: response in kind—
Part suicide, part payout, part rebirth.
Is it mere chance a cliff may be defined
As lover's leap, the real as down to earth?

Bargains Are by Definition Faustian

These are the years for mending what can still be mended.
Too many breaks already are not healed but ended.

As, when the equation's other half is gone
There can be no solution, and the one on one

That was the balance is a tipping of the scale
Toward being found forever wanting, horseshoe nail

Of battles lost, the gallows trapdoor sprung,
The weight of doom. I dangle on a too-sharp tongue

And too precise. The dust of gold, the empty pan,
The younger self strung up now tell me what they can:

Be civil to your former lovers, Kindly Poet.
If they have botched their lives there is no sign they know it.

If you have parlayed yours into a sort of Gounod
Kermesse you have paid a price. That much they do know.

But who's to say Mephisto's not seducible—
Where but on his own ground?—or that the crucible

All our bargains, not just this, return us to
Is not congenial, or that at least will do?

Having required more of our time, and shaped our ends,
Old enemies may mean more now than do old friends,

As if a bony finger, pressing down behind us,
Distorted values on the scales that so remind us.

Opposing Colonizations

Pasa thalassa thalassa

The continent has narrowed here toward Panama,
And where it narrows, rises. There are certain peaks
From which the oceans both are visible.

The Greeks once more are proven fallible: the sea
Is not, here, everywhere the sea. The one is blue;
The one is green; the nearer has the higher tides.

The White God vowing to return, if he could see
From this our eminence, might scorn the galleon,
Its raped Atlantic, and adopt the balsa raft:

A second coming out of Polynesia, trade
And not rapine the motive; or, more altered still,
Return as fire; from this volcano smite the land

In one blow, over time to make its soil more rich,
Or create diamonds in recompense for gold—
Geology as conscience money, sacrifice

Rewarded, if hereafter. On the heart cut out
There is not statutory limit; and, as haze
Turns gray the green Atlantic, and as cloud

Hides the Pacific altogether, what is clear
Is how the crater and the sulfur, if not Hell,
Are models of it, as are temples, as are mines.

Robinson Crusoe to Capt. Dreyfus

All islands are the Devil's in a sense:
The forcing ground of idleness, their threat
Of limits, of the inescapable.
Alluring at the first, they prison one
In solitude or make one realize
That in close confines two can be a crowd
And Friday seem a cellmate. Continents
At least have more than one landform to cross
And more than one time zone. And we who tally
Time by marks in sand or on a wall
Are proof ourselves that without mark or hope
It is a seamless sentence. Pardoned, you
Can think of this as some failed guillotine.
I, waiting rescue always, circle beach
To beach in hope of finding not the bare
Footprint of the unsought indigenous
But any trace of an invasion shod.

Energy Crises

Corpses of bats have been found on windmills at the
power plant in Altamont Pass.

—*Oakland Tribune*

Indifferent to, or unaware of harm,
Migrating bats divebomb the windmill farm,

Against a nonpolluting power source
A kamikaze strike to reinforce

Suspicion fossil fuels may be best.
Strip mine and drills belatedly contest

The loss of species with the newest trend
In solar heating, or—Midwestern blend—

Methane from cows or ethanol from corn.
To seek the flame the lovelorn moth is born,

Meaning he may attack selenium
On rooftops. And will revenuers come

To fuel pumps as to a whisky still?
Dung beetles to exhaust pipes? Boding ill

For spotted owls and such, as well it should,
The obvious renewable is wood

(Of course you have to wait a hundred years)
As too is whale oil. Once the mounting fears,

Threats, economic ups and downs grow thick
It's back to Ahab and to Moby Dick.

And do you, little bat upon the blade,
Further to make your point, biodegrade?

Or as the trust fund cases hug the trees,
Hang in until the global warming-freeze?

A Course in Sax Education

Created decades after all the rest,
Rogue instrument and uninvited guest,
The saxophone, as in the lyric, has
"A right to sing the blues," and not in jazz
Alone. It is the last low-tech new sound.
The cutting edge today is to be found
In synthesizers. Woodwind in design
But more a sounding brass, an androgyne
Allowed in symphonies on sufferance,
A solo sound in any circumstance,
Inflection paralleling human speech
As if the verbal were itself in reach.
So, just as electronic music skips
All intervention of the reed and lips,
And, although digital, of fingers, just
As jazz has no notation, all the dust
Of previous tradition Adolphe Sax
Blew quite away, and what his patent lacks
In subtlety it gains as prototype
Of music presently more Pan than pipe,
Always betokening its origin,
The Tenderloin it was created in.
Alderman Story, Earl and Blaze, poor street
Musician playing daily on your feet,
The sax for you is eminent domain
Between Parnassus and Lake Pontchartrain.

Production Values

What is it we accept as real?
The gaslight decades found no fault
In canvas flats or painted waves;
The 1930s did not cringe
At back projections as the world
In which screen heroes moved. For now,
Computer imaging persuades.
Tomorrow its spaced dots may seem
Virtual unreality
Or living actors virtual.
There is a test. The actual
Shows up the act for what it is:
Impersonation. Oedipus
No actor not a lunatic
Would take on in Vienna. Couch
One-ups the built-up boot, the throne,
As Ptolemaic marriage
Makes blinding oneself seem *de trop.*
No actress into middle age
Enjoys a scene with ingénues.
One cannot pass for young if youth
Itself is present, any more
Than a Kabuki heroine
Would be mistaken on the street
For woman. Did castrati sing
Convincing lullabies? The Globe's
Pubescent Rosalinds prolong
Careers by trained falsetto? Or,

At so to say the first crack out,
Give up? If blackface power passed
For true Black Power, minstrel shows
Might still be on the boards. Ahead,
If they join Actors Equity,
One must decide if clones have less,
Or have the same seniority
As those who gave the DNA.
Eternal understudies they,
Reality denies them role.
But Jekyll knows that Hyde is there,
And Hyde knows it is not makeup
By which in him we see ourselves.

Gowns by Adrian

Ignoring "period" as dress design by rote,
I made of shopgirls stately royals, gowns remote

From authenticity but so begemmed and stayed
As to allow the plainest actress to persuade.

No one would ever think my Mata Hari Dutch,
Or France's Queen on Viennese whipped cream too much.

The padded shoulder narrows hips; a trim of furs
Distracts attention from where body structure errs.

All through the '30s, frugal in their white and black,
Celluloid cried for color. I supplied the lack,

Or, if you like, finessed it, putting on the glitz:
Chain, bugle beads, lamé. So far as plot permits,

Egrets and ear drops. Mediaeval was my forte,
And wisely, Metro being first a feudal court.

I populated cunningly the Land of Oz,
Yacht clubs, ski lodges, back-lot Riviera spas.

And at the end, defecting to the Broadway stage,
I made of Camelot a modern Middle Age:

Adultery and spectacle, pride ripe for fall,
A land of Munchkins growing arrogant and tall.

The Garden of Yellow Jack

The tiger lily has a tiger's colors;
Something, maybe, of a feline's sharpness.
Its small sharp leaves are its bamboo, its Asia.
It lets us see in us a bit of sahib.

It is as if the smell of Easter lilies
Made one Palestinian a little,
Or in the hardening rosin of the pine tree
Already were the rosined bow, the measures.

Heat lightning, summer shower, steaming pavement;
And through the rising heat the rippling amber.
Rain, rain forest each are where you find them.
Asphalt and the sidewalk may be venue

Natural as any. Tiger, Tiger,
Burning bright, striated as if lightning
Striped a night, in changing to a lily
Sallow still, in quarantine's own color
Febrile on the vision, grace our fevers.

The Devil and Daedalus

What was the wish of Icarus?
To fly, or to be seen to fly?
What was the wish of Eve?
To know, or hope that, knowing, she could teach?
Do not presume that any end
Will cast a light on motive. Wax
Gone soft, explicit fruit enjoyed,
The sunlight conquers, and the serpent.
Threat subtle or threat obvious,
Free will is that to which, for praise,
The fabricating father frees.
A rib removed, the wing affixed,
Alike bespeak the patriarch,
As Icarus and Eve mean fall.
Flight, when it came, kept close to ground.
If knowledge comes, it comes in part.
Are they in league, the snake and sun?

Fashions of 1903

Except that, finally, it flew,
The Wright machine, at this late date,
Looks just as fanciful, as frail,
As sketches out of Verne's notebooks,
Or Leonardo's. One would say
The ancient Chinese airscrew toys,
Patents of Down East village cranks,
Ambitious steamer-glider schemes,
Professor Langley's "aerodromes,"
As projects are more plausible.
To pilot this construct or that,
No choice comes readily to mind.
Da Vinci's nude spreadeagled man?
In period, at least. A type
Of Richard Harding Davis, say,
To man the full-scale aerodrome?
(Its own mechanic was in fact
At such controls as Langley put.)
At throttle on the glider-steamer
Casey Jones, brave engineer?
The coin is tossed and Orville flies—
An anticlimax, insofar
As archetyping is concerned.
Nothing of new archangel there,
As surely man's first flight should hint.
Nor is the modest plane itself
A vehicle of Lucifer.
The narrow struts and linen wings

Somehow suggest arts Japanese:
The piecing of the minimal,
As in the later Wilbur, scarf
And helmet, goggles, stiff-necked pride
A bit of kamikaze shows:
Divine Wind as a coming mode
In flight's long history of styles.

The Last Cigarette Girl

In ever lower décolleté,
I work the tables with my tray.

If in my "Cigarettes, cigars"
There is no mention of their tars,

And though my manner hints at tips,
"Filter" does not cross my lips,

I'm finding out, as fewer smoke,
It is tradition I invoke,

Tradition being what lives on
When any need for it is gone.

Why is it "hatcheck girl" we say
Of one who puts no hats away,

Hats having followed Windsor knots
Toward Limbo after slow fox-trots.

A cry of "Acapulco Gold"
Might sell me out but see me fold,

The ringside tables being narcs,
D.A.'s, and vice squad. Needle parks

Have moved indoors? Hot pink hot pants
And Lucky Strikes are my one chance

At lasting till what goes around
Finds out I'm still around, a found

Sob story. Better, can I make
The talk show circuit if I fake

My sex? Transgendered trademark, morph
Into the Philip Morris dwarf?

Dance

In every dancer is a spastic trying to get out,
And getting out. The Martha Graham repertory brings,
Unseen as such, St. Vitus's life story twitch for twitch.
Outside the Rose Adagio the classic ballet seems
The reject of a dervish or a clean-and-jerk in tights.
A dance is footwork or is nothing, as the tango knows,
And hoofing. Get real, Martha. Ancient Greeks in brilliantine
Or Appalachians in taps each mock the origin.
To sound the forty whacks that shook Fall River hire Rockettes.

Free Trade in Mitteleuropa

As ceremonial as Roman rostral columns,
Trieste's two high flagpoles front the empty sea,
The city's abstract fleur-de-lis their latest crest,
A dark, heroic statuary as their base.
It is as if the Iwo Jima photograph
Had in a retroactive time warp straightened up
To be the '20s Fascist model. In the haze
That lifts the shining Adriatic out of time,
Makes it one surface with the spaces facing it,
One era with republics, communes gone before.
As likely as the empty shipping palaces,
Their architecture of Vienna-by-the-Sea,
There might arrive that skiff from *Island of the Dead,*
An unmanned Flying Dutchman of the stormless Gulf,
Or second raft of the *Medusa,* skeletons
On board as well as sprawling Second Empire nudes;
As in a bloodied operetta uniform
Franz Ferdinand was ferried north, as once
An Emperor of Mexico was floated home.
Tourism shows decline can be an industry
Like any other. Venice does not live on glass,
Vienna on the OPEC meetings. So Triest
Continues as Trieste, having just escaped
Becoming Trst. Outliving Yugoslavia,
Its lost "side door to Europe" waits the open door.

Where Is Gutzon Borglum
Now That We Need Him?

Boulders forming the silhouette were dislodged last week by
ordinary geologic forces. Embarrassing, as the famous image
appears on New Hampshire's souvenir coin.

—AP

The Great Stone Face existed as a face
In profile only. Should we in its place

Put up a one-man Rushmore in the round,
So literal that any meaning found

By some postmodern Hawthorne would be lost
In controversies over choice and cost?

The Profile had hawk nose and jutting chin
That one might contemplate New England in.

It was, full front, an overhang of rock
In which a symbolist would put no stock:

A naturally deconstructed text
Too jumbled to be dated or be sexed.

Generic Yankee, hero's portrait bust,
Whatever goes up on the mountain must

To make it onto any seal of state
Be too beyond contention to debate.

A Great Stone Jackie Kennedy, perhaps;
An Old Man of the Mountain under wraps

Until revealed as (You may put in here
Whichever rock star you just now revere).

Could no Onassis, God, cement or mortar
Prop up that image for New Hampshire's quarter?

Inventing the Subdivision

Humanity is done no credit if the Ark
Inertly floated and no more.
True, passages in Genesis do not remark
On keel and rudder, sail and oar,

But river dwellers ferry, deserts have their "ships,"
And Noah had the common sense
To onload camels, launch a dove on scouting trips.
And from day forty-one, immense

Profits accrue to who substantiate a claim
To any part of Ararat.
How many creatures to whom Adam gave a name
As mankind by the tiller sat

Eliminated one another in the hull?
A proto-Dodo, hopeless Crane,
Extinct as navigation exercised its pull.
Cheap flood insurance after rain,

The rainbow, though a promise, has as well its red,
Its hint of future tooth and claw.
But close ahead, toward which, by sail and knowledge sped,
The Ark is steering—development there in the raw—
Is real estate the pigeon saw.

The Last Elevator Operator,
or,
Mr. Otis Regrets

Level to level, floor to floor,
The elevator, as before,

Transports to buttons or to bows
Its button pushers. But suppose

The panel is not there; that I
Still man the lever, tout wares, pry

Stuck doors apart. My "Face the front"
Says all that automation won't.

It puts a human face on ups
And downs, the accidental stops,

The angst of the betwixt, between,
Of gravity's avenging spleen.

A buzzer can inform the blind;
By lighted numbers deaf are signed.

If sill and car do not quite meet,
The wheelchair's is a small defeat

Programmers did not contemplate
Or access laws ameliorate.

Of course, I could have saved the trapped,
Or any other handicapped;

In blackouts reassure; disrobe
The suffocating claustrophobe.

In cap of some Saint-Cyr cadet,
Mess jacket smart in gold and jet,

Unwilting crease of fitted pants,
Impassive in my rigid stance

I make a job thought of as dull
The hunting ground of Felix Krull.

Edith and Woody and Nancy and Ronnie

EDITH: I sheltered from his world a dying man.

NANCY: As I did. One must function as one can,
And I was daughter of a doctor. You . . .
"Ole Miss" a little out of time.

EDITH: How true.
The White House is the Old Plantation stripped.
No loyalty, no aid. A whited crypt.

NANCY: As keepers of the flame we kept the gate.

EDITH: Admit the Press and see them douse the grate.

NANCY: Did we succeed?

EDITH: You did. The long intrigue
Out of the East is done. As for a League,
That languished. Enemies are thick to meet:
The Kremlin or the Congress.

NANCY: Or the street.
Assassination, stroke; a few discreet
Releases as to state of mind or health

And we are held up to a charge of stealth,
Greed, power madness.

EDITH: Live a little while
Beyond the libelers and let that guile
Be your rebuttal. Once who pry are dead
Research will have to go with what we said.

Fishers of Men

Around the Gulf of Mexico—Campeche, Vera Cruz,
South Padre—it is Hemingway hotels that one should choose.

Hotels, that is, where deep-sea fishing types predominate,
Who will be out at sea in chartered boats all day, a state

Of grace for those who stay on shore, as we shall have the bar,
The pool, the poolside luncheon to ourselves, and the guitar

Quartet will spare us *La Paloma,* finding us too few
For so much effort. Nothing if not willing to let *you*

Be Hemingway, the waterfront photographer has scales
Of metric length and weight, so in his photos numerals

Will, being higher, more impress the good old boys back home.
In blazing lack of color, blinding as off polished chrome,

The sun goes down. The Papa clones return; the crew string up
Their catch to photograph. Too tired and too sunburned to sup

Tonight, tomorrow they'll be belting margaritas down
And seeking metric system taxidermists in the town.

Above the Gulf the moon is neither chrome nor polished. Pearl,
If you must have it, shadowed from inside. And, skirts atwirl,

Come ladies of the evening to the torchlit terrace tile.
Hooking implies too narrow focus. Wide net is their style.

Unto Temptation

Why is it that the Tempter is,
Himself, so little tempting? Faust
He offered youth, and Faust in tights
To Gretchen; tavern tunes for hymns
For Luther; Jesus on the heights
The citied wealth of all the world,
Which He refused. In human form,
As thief repentant, rival choice
For the Beloved Discipleship,
Might he have scored? The cloven hoof,
Unsightly horns, both miss the point,
In that they call for go-betweens:
Fruit, serpent, knowledge . . . One would think
That evil pure would have at least
Vain majesty and bold design:
A look of Lucifer, in shield
And shining armor. Uniforms
Are neither intervention, self,
Nor truth: are best foot forward, hoof
In cripple boot; and hornèd head
Fortunate Fall in Roman helm.
Hell being waterless, Narcissus'
Fate is not a threat should Vice
Give over its so frightful mien
To be seduction on its own
By virtue of a visage art
Avoids, and Milton carefully
Does not describe. It speaks as might

A looking glass. "Look at me, Cain.
You see the face of murderers
Who sleep well, certain of their course;
See, Judas, years of usury,
Yourself rich in the countinghouse.
Salt wife of Lot, see, grain by grain
Encrypted, segments of your past.
See, Herod, efficacious, praised,
The wisdom of infanticide."

Guidelines for a Cover Illustration

"Adventuress" is, as a term, this side of "slut,"
If only just. A sexist term and nothing but.

"Adventurer" touts heroism, if a sort
Whose purposes, in light of later ends, fall short

Of what Correctness calls for. As of now no one
Might be adventurer unless with knife and gun

And armor of the ethnocentric. Doubt, good works,
Children disqualify. The old way had its perks:

A native servant; chance to strike it rich; wear, more
Convenience than symbol, what the White Hard Core

Wear: jodhpurs and a real pith helmet. Low-rise jeans
On Peace Corps hips define what antihero means.

Nor does one quite see Vassar's Summer-in-Brazil-
To-Count-Endangered-Insects grist for Marvel's mill,

Or Hanoi Jane as Earhart. What screen type today
Would not appear ridiculous if forced to play

Above a score by Korngold? Astronauts are backed;
Adventure is the free-form, unsupported act

Predating Sputnik, NASA, Mission, or Control.
Its brash agenda, quick reward, its welcome role

Outside group think are envied by the orthodox
As the ability "to think outside the box."

It asks, of the society that it excites,
Exemption. Heroes do not haggle for their rights,

Which are the summit set upon, the banner placed,
The tiger in the sights, enchantresses embraced.

Crystal But Not Crystal Ball

Upon the sapphire is the light a star?
Who is to say it is not compass points,
Or non-Euclidean geometry
Upon the rounded blue? As sign a star,
The shining asterisk is star but less;
Is radiance without the consequence—
Astrology without prediction: twelve
In one, one fate and one mortality.
If you would have your charting different,
Examine then star rubies. Theirs is truth
Extrapolated from the blood, the flash
Of heat across the chill of mineral.
The East and West and North and South of love;
Its novel proofs, its parallels that meet.

Models

St. Petersburg, etc.

St. Isaac's in a photograph looks less
An Orthodox cathedral than a source
For most American state capitols:
The dome set on a colonnaded drum,
A pedimented portico. In fact,
Four pedimented porticos—East, North,
West, South—and columns not Carrara white
But opulent red granite. Not a touch
Taxpayers in the U.S. would approve,
Nor could they be consistently at ease
In presence of the giant church itself
And not the photo. Siege and weathering,
Neglect and riots, as in heavy mist
Distort Democracy's platonic form,
As if in Little Rock a late unrest
Had left its craters in the Statehouse steps,
Or insurrection pitted Charles McKim's
Rhode Island masterpiece. As in a sleep
Of Reason monstrously go by the wrecks:
New Hampshire gutted; Texas looking like
The Reichstag at the end of World War II;
Wisconsin razed for landfills in its lake;
Utah a vacant Zion on its hill.
If Baton Rouge and Lincoln skyscrape still,
Nebraska Deco, Long Regime and Speer,
Is it because Democracy has shrunk?
A legislature unicameral;

One man, one vote, and that the governor's?
Or is it that dictatorship rehearsed
Outlasts its fall and is alternative?

The Last Chaperon

I could have held down AIDS, and overpopulation;
Spotted fortune hunters; eased the trepidation

Of suitors rich but shy; promoted to advantage
The less attractive daughter; figured the percentage

By which her dowry should be raised; persuaded parents
Hairdressers and modistes may be their best adherents.

If I were duenna to the world I would inform it
Its urges can be dealt with, even as they storm it.

The checkrein to attraction is the eye averted;
Elopements are avoided by the house alerted,

Or—plucking fangs out of the eager adder—
Removing crucial rungs from every lover's ladder.

Desire is said to be insatiable. It isn't.
Self-interest can curb it; folly be imprisoned.

Obsession yields to common sense applied with rigor.
Failing that, there is the convent, or the trigger.

The most of theft is, finally, the key not twisted;
The irresistible, that which was not resisted.

Update for Francis Joseph

The quiet Danube eases past the quays
As though all meanings and all things which freight
Already had been borne away: a silt
For deltas, wreckage in the Dardanelles.
Restorers raise a time that never was,
Of ruins recent and without pathos,
As if some Japanese film studio
Put up Vienna's separate but equal
For the reptile monster to destroy:
High octane breath on Buda, panicking
The restaurants of Pest. Or as if each
Had been constructed as the other's folly,
The bridges in between them all their real.
What Romany the Germans did not gas
Are violinists in the restaurants.
One cannot know if Lehár stole from them
Or they from Lehár. It will be "Play, Gypsy"
When the Bomb has fallen. Centuries
Of occupation by the Ottomans
Have left at least a Turkish bath, intact
And functioning, a crescent on its dome.
Or is it sickle without hammer, Marx
As emblem put to rout? Crusades and creeds
Come each apart. The Double Eagle split.

The Passion of 1934

The decade turns at Oberammergau;
It brings the Passion Year. If who perform
Are largely Party members, who attend
Show no concern. Those who have seen before
Might notice this year more self-confidence
Among the soldiery, Iscariot
More focused on the specie rate; or see
In Caiaphas the makeup man's construct
Of Marx and Engels. Pilate seems this time
Not bureaucrat so much as diplomat;
Like Herod, deferentially subdued.
Almost by definition, one could say,
The mob is neither less itself nor more.
A little altered too, the Christus. Twice
Appearing in the role before, the Man
Of Sorrows adds morosely to the rest
His fifty years. Behind the pale blue eyes,
However, nothing is that was not there
Offstage. They are a sort of program note,
Unsatisfactory, as précis are.
Spectators must themselves extrapolate
How far the Via Dolorosa goes
And what will be its end. They've as a group
Some knowledge, insufficient, probably,
To show them how the Stations, one by one,
Confirm the irreversible. Someone,
A conscript—Simon the Cyrenian—
At any moment will appear, take up

The burden, change the ending. Will he not?
It cannot finish as it always has.
Except it will: Barabbas freed, two parts
Of theft and one of threatening the state.
Remember that the votive Play began
As gratitude for being spared the Plague.
Its repetition was to make secure
From pestilence the future. Up to now
That, absit omen, holds, although the blind,
The devil-ridden in the cast
Exist to tell us there are plagues and plagues,
Betrayal ever bolder in the text,
One kiss we have no understudy for.
Thomas will doubt, though never quite enough;
Peter continue to deny, in Rome,
And later, in the dock at Nuremburg.

Administrating

How many legionnaires would have been killed
Had Pilate not released Barabbas? Scores?
A minyan? None? The urgent mandate was,
Look to it Palestine does not revolt.
And not till Titus, did it. Faced with zeal
Astride an ass and credence waving palms,
Authority will drive its nails, add thieves
To render trivial the grievances,
Be more than ever thankful for the salver.
Centered in the center of the world,
Jerusalem whose navel is its view,
Upon a cross two others parallel,
Sedition distances itself from theft
Or promises it place in Paradise.
As if to whitewash washing of the hands,
Or pose in his own person "What is truth?"
The Procurator will go back to Rome.
Rome's judgments can, like any, be reversed—
If legionnaires are not the jury pool.

One Third of a Triptych

Why is it that in art the crosses of the thieves
Are lower than the other? Is positioning—
Between two thieves—not clear enough to spell out whom?
Are we in Egypt, where the Pharaoh was enlarged
And his attendants sized according to their rank?
One knows that Rome's intent was not to maximize.
Ignoring that on roadways crosses rose at heights
As uniform as streetlamps, art might well infer
The Empire would distort to keep its upstarts down,
As art itself apparently cannot accept
That real Godhood could ever be brought wholly down
To human level; that a jointly crucified
Mortality beside it, looking toward the promise
Or the scorn, need only look to left or right,
Not upward. "On the level" hints at truth.

Self-Guided Tour

1987

I, having seen Soweto thirty years ago,
When it was still Orlando Township, feel no need
To reinvestigate, and while my traveling
Companions are negotiating for a tour,
I tour the Jo'burg Stock Exchange: the *Ur*-Transvaal.
Anglo American, Crown Mines, De Beers . . . The quotes
Are writ in chalk; they speak in gold and diamonds.
Security is lax; outside on Hollard Street
Are Afrikaner guards, but in the gallery
For visitors I could assemble tear gas bombs,
Explosion of which might or might not jolt the shares.
The second Sharpeville riot hardly made a blip.
Three of the runners on the Floor are Indians.
Transvalers, one presumes, as they speak Afrikaans
Among themselves. The Traders are, predictably,
Illovo, Parktown, Wanderers. I know the look,
As I observed their blazers as they left their cars.
Their drivers seem to have, decades before cell phones,
Communication. How else draw up to the curb
On time? Diversifying one's portfolio
Means here no more than buying into platinum.
"Diversity" means so far only Boer and Brit
(At home it still means Johnny Reb and Billy Yank,
Though we do not admit it). Thunderclaps at four
Serve as the closing bell; the limousines queue up.
And, flashing in a darkened sky—Rand in the sky?—
Gleam out the golden veins; until the blue-white hail
Comes down in crystals up to seven carats. Where

Are you Antwerp, now that we need you? I waste time
Around the corner at a tribal herbalist's
(If you prefer, witch doctor's, or a dagga drop)
With kilted Cape Town Scots, two Bantu constables,
A probable shebeen queen, and a Durban imam,
To wait out limo traffic and the thunderstorm.
Wind chimes and ostrich biltong dangle by my head.

Report of the Monuments Commission

If Freedom has, or is, a goddess, should
Not Slavery have? Captivity *als Weib*.
As deity, no whips and chains; too much
Indicative of rare perversities,
And Slavery, over time, has been the norm.
Let her equipment be, like Justice's,
A balance. For the prisoner of war,
Death on the battlefield or servitude;
For youth, rebellion or conformity;
For age, the poorhouse or the family
(And which is Purgatory, which is Hell?);
For women without dower, take the veil
Or walk the street; for women with, endow
A nunnery and hope to wed for love
Or find no lover's not a gigolo;
For cotton pickers, seasons in the sun
Or codfish, God, and Boston consonants.
Put up in Washington along the Mall
An image of the Captivessa, borne
High on a ship of marble. Never ask,
Divinity, by whom your ship is rowed.
There's brooding Lincoln at the Mall's far end,
Brooding no doubt on how to keep in line
His border slave states. Let the goddess have,
For escort, gunboats, camels, you and me,
Sheikhs, maharajahs, and a Krupp or two.
Krupp workers' choice was, after sabotage,
A game of shower head roulette. And, too,

The Lowell mill girls, who could be "improved"
Or have a little fun, as Southerners
Were quick to see, and, not to spare the Jews,
Triangle Shirtwaist workers, unimproved.
Our prisoners political spill out
Their cell blocks, but could give up practicing
Marcuse, who lived himself in bourgeois ease.
For statuary goddesses there need must be
Consorts, and since we have become of late
Unwilling to distinguish Jefferson
From Belgian Leopold, let's add on both.
Upon the Mall the marches come and go,
Our sad charade. And from the great white dome
Freedom looks on, always *de haut en bas.*

Eclogue against Ecology

Fool's Paradise? And is there any other kind?
The fruits of Eden, we know, now, are largely rind,

And knowledge less a tree than some intrusive graft
That does not take. To know is not so much a craft

As it is exercise in self-deception: Eve
Or Adam, we embrace the Garden that we leave,

Attracted by the warnings put there to deter.
Deep down, it is the challenges that we prefer.

Hunting has more appeal than naming, and the name
Of any beast outside the gate is simply game.

From food to sport to murder is a seamless scale,
But if we break it we return to worm and snail

And that nude pair so bored they took up with a snake.
Cain's sons are gladiators; Abel's wield a rake.

If Eve has daughters have they taken to the street
From down the garden path? Had they a choice? Who eat

The fruit the pits will sicken. Checkpoint Angel, sword
Aflame, is gluttony the sin we backslide toward?

Soldiers Three in the Big Easy

Suspended during World War II, the Mardi Gras
Resumes in 1947. Will it be
Unrecognizable, as we ourselves may be,
Or so unchanged as to embarrass by its stance:
Its careful unawareness that a Feast of Fools
Has just concluded overseas. To reassure,
Parades are calendared as they have always been.
On Monday night is Momus, noon on Tuesday Rex,
And in the evening, champagne saucer in his hand
Instead of scepter, Comus. In a sleet of beads,
Infrequent hail of favors (none too new; one notes
"Made in Japan") in parsimonious largesse
The floats press on, cell phones and crowd control unknown.
Most uniforms one sees, however, are, like ours,
Not costumes. Navy whites are Argentines in port.
In chilly March as out of place as halter tops,
Not that they do not make the statement they intend.
Before the Boston Club's festooned reviewing stand
The Lord of Carnival Misrule will toast his Queen,
And his parade push forward, pressuring the crowd
Into the bars and restaurants. "It's hopeless, men,"
Our leader says. "We'll never find a table free."
"Let's go across the river," someone says, "Algiers
Is bound to be less crowded." So, wise veterans
Of harbor cities, well aware another side
Is always there, a parallel reality,
We take the empty outbound ferry.
                                        We return
Too late for Comus, having learned Algiers gears up

For Lent in its own way, as we for entering
Civilian life, the grim costume, the utter drag,
The forty days of 8 to 5 that never end.
So many decades on, my channel surfing done,
Sometimes, at midnight on Fat Tuesday, when the Courts
Of Rex and Comus meet at Comus Ball—TV
Is barred—I turn the TV off and think of Time
As sceptered, saucered god upon a float. A float
Papier-mâché, but fully Juggernaut enough
To grind down all who hope for favors, leap for beads.
Momus who mocks us, Rex who rules, and Comus, quick
To toast who wait the ferry with his empty cup.
The Pfc. who rhumbaed with the Argentine
Before he punched him out died long ago of drink;
The Corporal who ripped a passing halter off
Re-upped and vanished in Korea. I survive,
Rise early on Ash Wednesday, and do not repent.

Afterward

An earthquake jolts aside the stone;
The tomb is empty. An unknown

Informant says, "He is not here."
And so we have to go from there.

The highway to Emmaus leads
No farther than where hearsay breeds;

Outside the room where Thomas doubts
Others doubt also. Touch that routs

Such unbelief, if within reach
Of all of us, might have us each

Believer. To distrust the hand
Thrust in the side is to demand

Proof of so high a standard, sense
Plus Second Sight could not convince.

"The evidence of things not seen"
Is what the leap of faith has been,

But notice "evidence" is still
How we describe it. Past the sill

And sepulcher, threshold of lime,
For some brief forty days of time,

At random, not as if on cue,
Appears the missing to the few;

Comes in quite through the bolted door;
Eats; promises; is seen no more.